The Hockey Player Sonnets

The Hockey Player Sonnets

John B. Lee

PENUMBRA PRESS

Dedicated to the Golden Jet; to my father, who bought me my first New York Rangers Hockey uniform; to the Skatin' Scolors, who got me back into the game; to Roger, for 'Come Back, Jesus, to the Hockey Game of Life'; to anyone with whom I've ever played; and to everyone who has ever played and loved the game of hockey.

To my wife, Cathy, who lets me indulge myself in the local arenas late at night and puts up with me the day after.

© Copyright John B. Lee and Penumbra Press, 1991

Poems from the Hockey Player Sonnets have appeared in *Kunapipi* (Denmark); *B.S.P.S.; Poetry Halifax Dartmouth; Small Worlds; The Daily News* (Halifax); *The 1989 Nova Scotia Poetry Awards Anthology.*

'Dying on the Ice at 39 Is Hard' won First Place in the 1989 Nova Scotia Poetry Awards.

Published by Penumbra Press, Waterloo, Ontario, Canada, with the generous support of the Writing and Publishing programs of The Canada Council and the Ontario Arts Council.

Illustrations by Frank Woodcock.

Penumbra Press Poetry Series Number 26
ISBN 0 921254 253

Contents

Where will I winter when I am old

Oh where will I winter when I am old
And skates hang rusting in my outdoor shed?
Will my desire and my joy be dead
When all about the world is bleak and cold?
In muffled overcoat, gollashes rolled,
Slow moving down the street with gray-haired head
While all my friends have either died or fled
Left me here grumbling, ever unconsoled.

A sun shines in the waiting summer south.
Of tan and coconut and ocean wet
They'll tell me I should quit my northern house.
Perhaps these wags will stop and leave me yet
To marvel at the river's frozen mouth
Where season tells what I cannot forget.

Throw your Sticks in the Middle

LLLLLLLLLLLLLLL

⅃⅃⅃⅃⅃⅃⅃⅃⅃⅃⅃⅃⅃⅃⅃

Throw your Sticks in the Middle

❶
Three Period Game

Hockey Heart

His hockey heart
beats alone in the air
the surest player
on the pond of dreams
a boy
one skate boot on the bench
one on the foot
his fingers stiff
blowing his brittle hands
to get the frost out of the joints
always the last to leave
reliving the game, lost or won,
curing his mistakes
thinking of tomorrow
as if it were already yesterday
knowing that everything happens twice
once in the present
once in the past.

The Shinny Boys and the Gravel-Pit Fish

It was so cold
their teeth chattered
like milk bottles carried
from a truck to a door
but they sat in the pond snow
and tied their skates
as wind-hurled cries
took to the air
and clattered through the broken-stalked corn
till they were lost
like wing beats in a goose-killer's hands.

Oh shinny boys
are such racy things
their feet high-strung
and wild with wonder.
Yes, what the gravel-pit fish must think
beneath this topsy-turvy aquarium
where they strobe
the icy depths quick-flicking fins
in the mutter and scratch of muted noise.

A Game of Shinny in the Moonlight

Moonlight
pours like skimmed cow's milk
down the sky
to where the shotgun crack strikes
half-blind
at the black disk that slides
a frozen mile
along the creek top.

Boys blur
and scribble out
to where it leaps ditch grass
cocked over
and frosted
or bumps on the waxy nubs
cut by wind like a king's seal on the surface.

These bandits come and go
in the swirling cloak
of gothic night
chasing the plot of a maiden-moon
passing through cloud
like ghosts through a hanging veil.

When I was a Boy and the Farm Pond froze

When I was a boy
once every winter the farm pond froze
wide as a field from fence to fence
we'd go down with skates, puck and stick
and play in the burning wind for days
the ice slithering with cracks
under our weight
seeping at first with water, then
collapsing in dried hollows where the furrows
cut tiny valleys
in the plow-rolled earth
till the game shrunk to such boundaries
of ruin
we could hardly turn between the evaporating kingdoms
of snow-boot goals.
Then one terrible day the whole wreckage
broken on the knuckles of frosted clods
would lie fallen like a puzzle tossed in the air.
That was the last of the generous mornings.
The last of the pond
groaning like a fat man's bed
when the wind turned suddenly cold and ordinary
and the snow scattered in filthy patches
stippled with dust.

Canine Pylons

When I play hockey alone with my dog
in the moonlight
I'm Gretzky flashing circles round
a canine pylon.
He's there paw-splayed
turning and scrambling
and falling
and yelping for his skated-over tail.

But when he gets it
he can really carry the puck
in his mouth
and off the pond
into the snow
where he drops it
and it makes a round slot
plunking through onto frozen earth.
A dark needle in a white haystack
acres from the ice edge.

All the 'Get it boy, get it boy,'
doesn't mean a thing.
He knows he's scored.
And somewhere
Foster Hewit has lost his voice from shouting
over barking dogs.
And somewhere Scott Young
is phoning in the scoop.
And somewhere dogs are laughing.
Somewhere that skates don't matter.
Somewhere that Wayne Gretzky
is just another pedestrian
walking four inches above the pavement.

Pneumonia Deliriums, or
why I didn't play Hockey as a Child

I lay the last time
with my forehead hot and dry
thinking this must be how a person dies
diving in the infected flaming liquidly self
beneath fever's figment of wings that flutter
at the window casements
like the wind-whipped hair of little girls
my small dark fists untightening to catch each coin of light
as one by one bird shadows
burn the edges from the room
and I float
in swimmy lampglow
that shines like an egg yoke broken in water.

But I hold the smudged world real
until the couch resumes its obviousness
and pain recites
the contours of my flesh.

Every winter for seven years
I stroked the same cat
in the same closed parlour
with the same mother
whose same hand lit palm-up on my forehead
like a curled wet bang.
Too young to hold such frequencies of heat
my lungs unpuckered bits of greenish phlegm
and when I coughed
my soul trembled like a curtain
that's forgot the window it was meant to mask.

But when the hideaway doors
finally blinked open in the wall
every molecule in me jumped
to the rushing foodsmells
and my father paper-rustling in the den
or a kitchen chair dragged over old Tom's corner
and the dog whining at the back shed
claw-stroking the door for want of company
with my uncle searing a pot bottom in the dishwater.

For these transparencies of love
there are enough reasons
while other boys could streak about the world
erratic comets purblind with straying light
the illness let me lay a while
and count them one by one.

Watching the Roaring Twenties
on Saturday Night

i

Pinky had a pretty mole
but she was gun-moll tough
and speakeasy loose
in the criminal night
where booze flowed
into the glassy scherzo of barroom chitchat.

And every Johnny was troubled by the violin case
carried in by the spats-dandy thug
knowing anytime a tommy
might coin its fatality from within
stuttering little ink-blots of blood
into some punk's best pajamas
with coffins of silence
whenever a gun was pulled
every heart thumping
like a jazz drummer's best paradiddle exploding
into a jangling highhat
lifting the stiff white-as-quicklime
shirt collars with a single gulp of fear
and then the verdict rattled out
like a quick-spanked cymbal
stitching a crooked judgement
like bad mending and the stuff of life
spilled everywhere
as if death were a furious painter
with nothing but red on his palette.

ii

My father always made popcorn
and sat in his easy chair
drinking the only beer I ever saw him drink
his mind fixed on the program
like the cross-hairs of a sniper

and my nose
bumped by the exquisite bubbles

of a cold cocacola,
my fingers silky with butter,
I joined him there in the sacramental Saturday night
drawn inside the manly cabal
that never quite included my sister
or my mother

most especially when the hockey game came on
with the excitable Danny Gallivan
marking the play
like a breathless adventure.

Then my sister disappeared
and mother fell asleep
hey eyes gently closing like music-box lids
in a baby's room.

iii

I watched because
perhaps I could divine some secret
of my maleness concealed from me
by the god of sport
and because I felt
to do otherwise would be to snub
my father's perplexing need
to share the spectacle.
So I watched
the room, and I watched
the commercials 'Hey Mable,' 'Put a tiger in your tank'
and I watched
the sweat trickle from a player's chin
in the studio lights
between periods
and listened carefully to the broken english
and the choppy exhausted
exhalations of each winded syllable …
all of which held more interest for me
than the actual game.

And what do I give my own sons now
troubled with the need
to enter my world.

Do they suffer my own afflictions,
so private, a poet's like a captured spy.
Do they long for the gift
of my spirit touching theirs,
confined as it is in its solitary cell.

Do they live just beyond
the rim of predilections
I construct like a labyrinth of bubbles
on an idiot's lip
puzzled by the delicate surfaces
bursting with hope
round the air-tight seal
of a father's heart.

Pity the Boy who believes

Pity the blade-seized soul
whose father stamps out the cold
and blows over his coffee cup
at six every morning
when the winter sun is pale as a stone-fed yoke
and the parking lot snow
crunches like breakfast cereal under his boots
all the way to the rink.

Pity the winded boy who dreams of glory
and would play in the dark without bread
when the moon's thin light drapes
the pond's starved reeds that thread the frozen shallows.

Pity him for those his best years
when his young life was all possibility.
Pity him for the bitter years to come,
awful with could-have-beenness
that makes tomorrow's sun
so large, even the stars shrink down
to insignificance and disappear.

Table Hockey

Little men turn
little ballerina men, swivel
click, click, whack, whack,
puck careening, up on its wheel
rolling on its rim
or cat's eye glass
scrolling a rippled blue peril.

Boys' hands agitating the pen springs
worry the slots
up and down the press-board ice
click, click, whack, whack
wearing a groove in the thumb
a hay man's blister
one shaft end taped where the knob's gone
AWOL in a furnace grate
one winger sluggish
so he swings stiff as a café door
one headless centre
his stick buffing the paint as he goes
wicky wacks a ramrod line
and slaps the wide goal tender
then spanks a pass that slashes
off the boards
and drops in the slot
like a juke-box nickle.

A cheer rasps the air
a boy's voice sandpapered
by a Christmas afternoon
with his favourite cousin.

Playing the game board
that tortures dining room veneer
like screw drivers
and bumping the tea wagon
so the crystal jumps and jiggles together
as if every glass were toasting a bride.

These were the days –
the tournament days
one hand on the goalie's flat manipulator
one hand scooting the knobs
bloody knuckled with the need to be fast
and careless of the hurt
till you slammed a nail
so it enveloped the metal to the cuticle.
These were the days –
the Christ-loving days
when clock hands spun
like a kissing bottle
that God set swirling
and it stopped every sweep
pointing directly at you
though you hardly ever paused long enough
to feel the grace.

The First Time each Season

The first time each season I
twaddled skate hasps
and
stepped on the ice
after a long hot summer on the beach
my hockey equipment burning
at the straplines while I stroked
woozily on the strange surface
till I learned to glide again

and the first time
the puck snapped its weight
against my blade
it dragged like a dry swallow
for an instant
then melted into useless ballet swivels
that spun off the tip of my stick

and the first time
I gained the bench I sat gulping air
like an upended coke bottle

and the first time
the game finished
in the last shortening day of summer
we fell in our stations
in the dressing room
the whole sweaty place pumping its musk
in the nostrils
alive with the sweet sorrow of overness.

When Jamie hits the Ice

When Jamie, the bookseller
talks about playing hockey again
after all these years away from the game
I see the ghost of a child
in his eyes.

Not a ghost
of smoke rising from a movie-house cigarette.
Not a ghost
of milk squeezed
between two panes of glass.
Not a ghost
of moon shadows
lost in cloud.
Not a ghost
of a nightgown whipping its empty sleeves
on a midnight clothesline.

No, more the taste of an apple
when the apple's gone.
More the heart of a story ten-times told
that plays itself out in the mind.
More the trace of a dream that wakes you
under pale skies
to the sound of a cat
padding the kitchen linoleum.
More a reed-wand waving beneath ice
after the first freeze
on an old farm pond
while you lie on the surface
feeling the cold that creeps along your chest
and burning palms
your face pressed close to look
at disappearing things.

The Myth of Cohen

after an NFB film

This poet denies the game –
of Peter – the cock will crow thrice
before the sun jumps
like a ready player over the boards
and his call will last for a time
then unwinding slow like a wet curl
gone heavy with rain
and all the easy energy explodes
because truth
can no longer be trusted
then Cohen rides the camera lens
shambling the streets of Montreal
like an old man in slippers
pretending to be young
he shuns the great Canadian possibilities
for a thick-tongued angst
and all the high-wire birds sing hosannas
by a lonely cheap hotel
with the snow as white as a trucker's undershirt
dropped on gray walkways
weakness in the body, studied frailness in the frame –
these are power too.

Laurence came to play

When Laurence came, he came to play.
So he dropped each poem
in the well of a mind
like a coin
it nerved in circles
drawling the depths
till it bumped full-bottomed
on its drowned face in the fishless dark,
but when Laurence came, he came to play.
He rushed from the reading room
like a stream of air
from a cookstove door
and raced for the ice
where he touched his frock
like a priest his chasuble
and dressed for the game
he struck out full force in his stride
and swivelled like an easy banker's chair
for the hockey net
and whacked the puck for glory
past the broad pads and grim-as-Africa face.
It went deep as a grave for a dog
where the winter that set
this harp on its side
and tuned these man muscles
for their fastness and grace
also broke with silence and the dreary done
of heart that had hummed
like an instrument thumped in its case
caught scarlet in its cage
out-poemed the poet
who carried it home.

Last Night it snowed

Last night it snowed
and the world is deeply packed

so I head out early
with my little shovel
and cut cubes big as beer cases
in the driveway
which grows by slow gray sections
towards the faraway curb.

All morning I lift these measured die
and tip them one by one over the chain-link fence
for I need to tunnel out the car
... hockey's at three ...
and I need to tunnel out the car
... I need to tunnel out the car
blinking like a troubled mole
I look at the milky winter sun
then forge my body forward
bent and straightened bent and straightened
like a wire someone's trying hard to snap.

I will suffer
the imperatives of weather
no less than boys who'll work three hours
cleaning an outdoor pond
for the thrill of an afternoon of shinny
where under a cold white moon
they'll rush and chase and clip
until worried mothers call them freezing home
their nostrils glued with ice.
And so I sweat and grind my shovel mouth
through inner songs
that play my breath
till I am walking in between two hospital walls
of snow and heaving at the door of my garage,
thus are such obstacles to the game
a stony madness for this tired Sisyphus
to push aside
and find another Lazarus revived within his skin.

Best the Pond froze on a Windless Night

Best the pond froze on a windless night
when the cold was as still as a palace guard
no vague corrugations
nor breeze-bubbled grass
to interrupt the stride of skates
slashing arcs for the fish to read.

Even now
when I walk with my boys
toe tapping the fragile wafers
that skin these pathway puddles
I grow glad hearted
when I see a surface stretched out smooth
as a queen's tablecloth
and I think of someone gliding
like a licked finger across a mirror
then the world has its moments of kindness
that force the cynics
to shore up their best arguments
against joy.

The Connection

I was but a little lad
when I heard the news of how
the roof had collapsed heavy with snow
on the small-town Ontario arena
crushing the game within
on the suddenly perishing boys.

I'd watched my mother pour wheat flour
from the cab-yellow sack
on the flat board
to make pies
later all those still cherries
trapped beneath the upper crust
like the tiny hearts of dead children
while the white dust
that powdered her hands was washed away
in a milky swirl ...

but I made no connection then
though I make one now.

❶ ❷
Three Period Game

Sitting in the Grays with the Blues

Outside the Gardens before the Leaf's game
icicles clatter down
like hardware too heavy for a nail
the sky
is a vague and dissipating ghost
with snow falling softly
in whispered secrets
to the gutter fungussed with brown slush
by a sewer-grate kettle steaming in the street
where chestnuts roast over smuts
on a glass wagon
while comers and goers struggle against insignificance
puffing like knocked-together chalk brushes
their bodies wrapped against winter
like fragile postage
pass scalpers barking their commerce
making tawdry deals
in the petrol-stinking night.

Inside the gardens a man fingers his buttonhole
and climbs the Escher nightmare
past the R.E.M. of vertigo
where gravity loosens its grip
and he might slide down air.
From there he can watch the game
his eyes falconing the puck
while all around him
the fans are clucking fox-jawed
some dangerous with disappointment
some overwhelmed by coffee
brood about the exit rush
and the plot jump of weather going on without them,
meanwhile snow gathers to moss the parking lot
and ice knits its crooked scarves of traffic
where cold wields its authority over engines
that strangle awake under key clicks
and light blinks that probe the edgeless dark
and muss for an hour or two
beyond the groaning arches of the building
where kids stray-cat with crazy hair

and cigarettes thrown away lit
lie like whip marks on cement
and bums drink from bag ends
in a sick wrinkle by a doorway shelter.

Still later with the night-numbed clock
running like a dreaming dog
on the empty street
the first car away moves
tiny like the growing tip of a root
into the life source
of another city, another home.

Drinking with the Boston Bruins

When a girl I knew
was drinking in a bar with a friend
the entire Boston Bruins hockey team
fresh from an 'exhibitionist's' game –
or some such thing –
as it were
and being self-impressed and youngish studs
or so they fancied
came bursting in and began to chat and flirt
in every direction.

Now, there was one, a playboy in his own mind,
trying hard to make the most of his moustache
while my friend, desperate with ennui,
glancing down the long table
of jolly men,
spied not a single interest in the lot,
and tuned out the vain one
who prattled on about himself as if she were a sportscaster
hanging on his every word
the hour crawling by like 6 o'clock Toronto traffic,
until she left the table
walking in the barlight
that dripped in the snoozing smoke
where it whisped like cow breath in February
out of that place and into the sky beyond
still they locked on her black zeroes
and made a lazy man's puzzle
out of her, since 'what's a woman for but fitting into'?
but it doesn't take all day
for a day to happen nor for the early night
to pass, and make a pass in passing
incomplete, the puck, the period, the back of the net
and scoring such voluptuaries
as the game supplies.

The Trade that shook the Hockey World

When Gretzky went to L.A.
my whole nation trembled
like hot water in a tea cup when a train goes by.

Something about Hollywood and hockey.
Something about Canadians in Babylon.
Something about gold and the gilded blades of grace.
Something about kings and the great republic.
Something about titans and the golden gods.
Something about the myth of boys and the truth of men.
Something about beer in the holy grail.
Something about the commodity of the human heart.
Something about the fast life ...
fast food, fast cars, fast women, and a fastness.
But mostly something about moving too fast in time.

Tripped by Andy Bathgate

Hockey players, using such devices as they have,
will trip you when your back is turned,
so it's little wonder
that when we won our brief glory
with the gray-haired NHL

Ron Ellis swishing backwards
like a bonspiel sweeper
humiliating D who rolled after him
first this way then that
like a ship captain's breakfast egg
while they outloped us
breathing slow and easy as unstoppered wine
no matter how we chased the puck
we were but pups out after butterflies
and my own moment came
when in the long shadow of a play
Andy Bathgate looking still
like the old bee-hive syrup hockey picture
from my boyhood
slipped his stick in the slot of my blades
and yanked me from my pins
so I wooshed to the ice
like something too slippery to hold
and he grinned down at me
as if to say
take that one for the archives
for being tripped by Andy Bathgate
is a kind of history too.

Under a Hockey Moon

for Tim Horton

The fast car blasts against the abutment like a Technicolor
sneeze
under a hockey moon that shines
behind christening-dress snow clouds
against the priest's cassock
of a winter night.

Later, ambulance bleeds a swirl
tracing the dark highway
to the soul
marooned like a veil
snagged in the metal husked
over concrete slabs.

How many times must a cheek in the dust
be a purse for a life unspent,
and how many times
must promise be broke
by clay-locked bones
and how many ghosts
must stray like a rasp in pure light
before God opens his large hands
to catch one sparrow
not to prove a miracle
but to save us from the need.

John Lennon and Yoko Ono cheer for
Gordie Howe as an Out-take

From The White Album

Number nine ... number nine ... number nine ...
number nine ... number nine ... number nine ...
eeoway ... eeoway ... eeoway ... RIOT!!!!!! RIOT!!!!!!
number nine ... number nine ... number nine ...
if we ... number nine... if we... number nine...
if we... number nine ... if we get naked ... RIOT!!!!
!!!!RIOT!!!!!!!RIOT!!!!!!!! eeoway ... eeoway ...
eoway ... number nine ... number nine ... number nine ...

At Ilderton Fair

My uncle sat shucking elderberries
with a famous hockey referee.
Both men were shepherds,
but only one was expert here and now
fast husking the torn-off branches
by the bleating pens
so the fruit rained from his blue hands
like water out of wet sheep's wool.

The loser was amazed by the other's skill
for all afternoon he'd worked
grooming the plants like a careful father
combing out his daughter's tangled hair
and had little more than a tea cup or two
though the berries were perfect each unto itself
a flawless unbruised gem
even a jeweler would be proud to set upon his tooth.

Then my uncle had come
bringing his big hands for the fast harvest
and in an instant
had them splashing the berries on their bellies
and spawning on a tarp
in a flood of excellence
jigging up to his ankles in their ripe hum
he smiled
thinking – this is an event –
even the absence of a camera cannot deny –
this is a happening –
this is another kind of hockey game –
and I am skating wild and free
like the mind upon a memory.

Falstaff as a Hockey Goalie: taking the Edge off

He stands in the black galaxies of the net
swishing left and right
where the whole pulsing universe
hums like a whip in the flesh of God.

And while scalding disks
bite his leather
in the mount and settle of their flacking hour
he wags like a lover's hammock –
his skates swabbing and weightless
as a hanged man's ticking feet.

But sometimes his nerves betray him
too fast, too slow, might
jitter a muscle like a fly-bit horse's rump.
So before the game he drinks
to get the edge off,
to slur his conducting arm
that rocks his open hand
or nurse the fever from his brow
or soothe his gut
calm him down to smoothness
the way a breakwall tames the sea
and thus he splays and shuts
and dives and clicks and flicks
within the tiny kingdom of his goal
where spine jerk's a bucking ram
and the thing that is the game
untwists with time
and flattens like a crumpled note
to read the noble madness of what's done
and drink a little more
until the print unsnarls
and the brain waves a sweet farewell
like a dreamy wife scented into the waning mystery.

Prince Hal on Skates

for Bobby Hull and Bobby Orr and Bobby Anybody

Some can weave the lonely dangers
with golden hair.
A silk-scarfed dancer
sky-flirting with the gods
strikes the flint of bliss
sparking blue fire
with an arc-welder's best seam
left invisible as a healed-over scar
on a baby's wrist.
Oh, there are entire orchards
would cast their blossoms down
snowy with delight
and even the last squinting fragment
of antediluvian good will
would spectrum in their dreams
while doves crowned their pillows
with an olive-scented kiss.

Even death grows dizzy with desire
when they lie like sleeping maidens
in the grave
and their dust upon the wind
it too is fantastic with light
like cloud-chamber physics
scintillating in the eye of God.

When Bolingbroke usurps the Hockey Helmet of a Fallen King

What new Bolingbroke will come
to pinch the crown
with all the fat complacencies of glory gone
from those once God-loved prodigals
– good boys, bad boys,
with knees like barn hinges torn in a storm
or hair gray as ten-day old bread,
targets for the quiet reproach of time
every one
slowing like the recognition of a long-forgotten friend.

The past sits
like a foot chewed off in a frost-jawed trap
when all that remains
are the days
to drag leg-clumping up a flight of hills
and the blood spoor that
leaves its blight beaded in the snowy trail
like berries dropping frozen from a sieve.

We have enough too-young crownless kings
to populate a ghoulish room
and stories to tell
with stories yet to come
jaw wagging
like a mockish set of dentures
in a dentist's hand.

Hotspur on Skates

When he would skate a prosperous plot upon the ice
and tip the black coin thus and thus
as great magicians do
knock untitled crowns usurping all their grace
with theft and palm a corner
like a tribute to his watching maid
while every single minute hushed itself
all eyes amazed like roses by the sun
where they open like the skirts of summersaulting girls
and skate will take a blade
for Blade
the low predicament of weightless gliding harmony
the way a note is found upon a slide trombone
then found again
but when he is bumped outside the groove
then comes a quaking which unstudies
his ear and pitches him like a canker touched
that makes him leap to pluck
the other's weedgrowth of a pate
by drowned-in-crimson hands
and make a carnival of rage there on the spot
with peevish swatting as with bee-stung fools
who stand upon a meadow nest
and flail or sit on pismires with honeyed bread
and pinch themselves to death
for fear they'll lose a bite.
And striking out, this Henry Percy of the rink
'er he'll admit to wrong
and as aging swiftly dries a swiftness from a joint
he'll rage and look for rage
before he'll face the looking glass
and see how he sizzles
for an instant
then like spit in flame he is consumed.

Short Shift

His HEART bangs in his chest
like the bottom of a salt shaker
when the salt is wet
huffing and puffing and positively post coital
he settles his frame in fat
his spine like a pearl necklace smuggled in cold cream
he begs to be left alone
to breathe himself alive
this short-shift Falstaff, dropped there like a sack of cats
on the hockey bench.

Though he is young
and drunk with youth
would lift his fulsome self
and strive his rabbit-thumping HEART
to death
or swear a breathless oath above his meal
before he supped
so gone is he with the game
but his boyhood brought him heavy portioned
to this untimely gadzooks
upon the pine
and he must quit or die.

By the Norwich Arena I sat down and wept

At the Norwich arena
the Junior C hockey game
has just ended
and the stand's mob
              is a writhing insurrection.
Everywhere you look the rage
is boiling like a cowboy's laundry.
Already the players have leapt the boards
to grapple on the ice below us.

Here and there
someone in the stands shoves a stubbled jaw
in my face,
or some shrew shrieks wielding her handbag
like a grief-crazed ninja's numchuck.

And me, all I want
is to leave
this roar of the madding crowd
so I take my wife's hand
and we thread the riot
with a circus of fists leaping over our shoulders
till we pass the confection stand
and out into the parking lot
where the night lies open
like a bandage lifted from a wound.

The next morning while a spring breeze
blows its nails in thin grass
we hear how the visiting team
boarded the bus
with the aid of a police escort...
how they formed a phalanx
and wedged through the rabble
in the blood light
that swivelled from cruiser tops
like surgeon's water swished away slow
fists thumping the side of the bus
as it moved
groaning for the road

dragging its gray exhaust
with one or two
exposed buttocks dangling from a window,
the whole town shouting
under a beautiful moon
pale as the brow of an antebellum Southern belle.

❶ ❷ ❸
Three Period Game

Terrifying Metaphors

Perhaps for a fleeting moment when I was ten
I believed that jocks grew up
and that there would come a time
when I could be incompetent at sports
without the pseudo-manly ridicule
of the dexterous body-perfect boys
who populated the playing fields
or my semi-tragic youth.

That I might out-distance the harangues
of the ball catchers, and the holler
of puck slappers, and the yammer
of pigskin kickers
who would eventually panty-raid the universe.

But
now that I am in my thirties
and would have thought
it impossible for such ideas
to survive the knocks of life
I finally realize
that jocks are jocks are jocks
facing the long monotony of a slow decline
locked in aging bodies
which go unrecognized
mocking them
with terrifying metaphors.

The Hockey Player Sonnets

for Al Purdy

i

What about them Leafs, eh!
(expletive deleted*) couldn't score an (e.d.) goal
if they propped the (e.d.'s) up
in front of the (e.d.) net
and put the (e.d.) puck on their (e.d.) stick
and the (e.d.) goalie fell asleep
and somebody (e.d.) yelled, 'SHOOT THE (e.d.) THING!'
   (E -E-E-E. D-eeeeeee.!!!!!!!!)

ii

(e.d.)!! this (e.d.) shower's (e.d.) cold.
who the (e.d.) flushed the (e.d.) toilet?
give me the (e.d.) soap.
hand me that (e.d.) towel.
has anybody got some (e.d.) shampoo.
toss the (e.d.) over here!
thanks. what's this (e.d.) pansy (e.d.)?

who brought the (e.d.) beer?
toss me one. stop throwing that (e.d.) snow.
you could lose an (e.d.) eye.
and so on …

iii

What do you mean you don't watch sports on TV.
Why the (e.d.) not?
Haven't you got an (e.d.) TV?
What the (e.d.) do you watch?
What the (e.d.) do you do?

Read! ! ! – who the (e.d.) wants to (e.d.) read!
too much like (e.d.) thinkin'.

there is much (e.d.) laughter at this.
and so it goes –
'what about them Leafs, eh …'

                              * *hereinafter referred to as 'e.d.'*

Night was the First Thing to fall when the Hockey Team went to Buffalo to see 'The Great One' play

Night was the first thing to fall
it
staggered like a sweaty drunk
on the close horizons
then
tumbled down the dusky edges of itself
angled above
the buildings of Buffalo ...

then Stink
was arrested in the Aud
then Biff 'nd Billy
picked at a big cop's ego
till his gun jumped on his leg
and tempers got hot
as cheap cafeteria coffee
then Paly
struck his fat ass
(bump-bump-bump)
on three cement steps
from walking on air
then Skip slapped the stranger's head in front of him
so the skull rattled
like a cloth-wrapped bell
then Tiny went
for the cleavage of a 'babe'
with 'boobs' the size of fancy hotel pillows
then Horse picked out the largest mesomorph in the stands
and threw an empty paper cup at his 'lady'
so it careened off her hair
like big confetti
then mulling and herding
they went wild in after the game
'Stop and Go'
crushing foaming half-quaffed unbought beer cans
ripping up chip bags and hurling them
in the aisles,

squashing Twinkies,
shouting, 'Only in America
can we get away with this shit, man.
Land of the brave, home of the free.'
then running away before the cops would come
then rumbling home in the bus rain
with the night as wet
as the green blat of grass-fed cow
a few philosophized
hockey
while one brute
led a stentorian chorus of 'the S and M man'
ten guys knew the words
recited them
like ten vulgar Hamlets
slumming in Elsenor
a few skirmished on a road-jarred patch of gravity
while an hour passed like a kidney stone
in the urine-coloured headlights
therein I was the second thing to fall
though I was sober and staggered
only in my mind.
red

No Body Contact

No body contact hockey
is like no body contact love.
It doesn't exist.

A half-intended check
a comedy of gestures
exploding on the endboards
like a barroom chair
or an elbow in the cage
eyes fluttering like nervous budgies
till the stick comes flashing there too
tick tick tick
tormenting.

And then there are the revengers:
'I don't get mad;
I get even!'
neanderthals the cool arena
and garlic belching excitable mutilations
travel the bench in mumbled justice fantasies.

Hapless targets glide by
exposing their throats
like doomed kings or submissive wolves
and the torn rose petal of a bruise
supplicates a butt-end on the voice box
or the hand begs to be chopped from the wrist
like a kind of harsh Islamic judgement.

And the referee
his ears wet
with the hydrophobia of questionable calls
or this thumb flattened and tooth marked
on the cuticle
is finally drawn into the catfight spin
sorting out the firstness
in this parable of single socks.

Industrial League Hockey

Leaning against the factory wall
– victims of the night,
their smoky breath hanging like cut lamb's tails
in the air.
One rattles wax wrap open
to liberate a dry cheese sandwich
while others grumbled
by the engines groaning in the green-glass light behind
admiring the way the trucker
threads his long load backwards through the needle's eye
of a doorway
that sighs open exuding steam
like the slow and sexy exhalation of a movie star.
And it is men such as these
unjailed by their off hours
that come to play
and from the first angry moment
of their swarming
through the door onto the ice
I knew there would be trouble
from the burly cluster of their workworn knuckles
bristled with black hair.

One fellow wearing a helmet high
on a skull-bone brow
as thick as a cheap cafeteria dinner plate
came racing
his derailed motors
intent on some kind of mutilation
with all 12 seasons of eating concentrated
to sustain the monogrammed pig-iron slabs of his pectorals
smelted in the forge of a big-wombed dam
with a vigorous appetite
and forearms like a Spanish pirate.

These he hurled at liberal fancies
occasioned by a world-weary mind
to scribble
a confession concerning swans
in a river
and astonishingly alone in the inclination
to think of the grace
before the meat.

Christmas Hockey Game,
Faculty versus Students

for Al Purdy

Here on this ice
we skate,
each year
a little older
each year
a little grayer, a little slacker in the gut
and slower, as if age were a drug
with a long half-life
releasing minutes into the blood stream
till finally we will be sluggish
as smoked bees.

And each year the kids come at us
younger, fresher, stronger, more full of life,
always the same joke at the blue line,
always the same faces
off and rushing the net.

Some day we'll seize like rusty shears
or drawl like strings
winding down from unhooked kites
the puck will leap
and pass through insubstantial cavities
like a bird through light fog
where we look all cloudy
vapored as we are upon exhausted frames
and whispering ghosts of former selves
but there too
the ghost of a happy boy.

The Firehall Blues

We cure the firehall blues
with booze.

After we've hung our skates to dry
like ripe skins
we talk about accidents.
Checks,
slashed faces, eyes carved out of skull's knot holes.
One year
Al saw a boy die on the ice
his jugular cut
and pumping red.

But mostly we talk about scoring.
The easy grace
in the best of us
swivelling into perfection
only then
when the puck arcs past a shoulder,
or slides cool and swift
along the ice
to tangle in the netting
like a hard black fish
that darts of its own accord.

We get drunk
on victory
smashed
on defeat
and when we go home to our wives
tired and drained with the telling
of the same stories
in as many ways as we can conjure
we go with the knowledge
that we will pay dearly tomorrow
for the glory
we hooked tonight.

'I don't wanna hump, I jes wanna dance'

What I like best about him, this 'hockey player,'
is his respect for women.
All the 'vulgar talk' aside
beneath it
he'd ride out on a cold morning
with sharpened objects
trained against every daughter taker
a good father could find,
or after the 'girlie' jokes
had died on his lips
he'd look dreamy-eyed over a drink
across a candle-lit table
at some 'chaste maiden'
burning white in the pure fire
of virtue's incandescence
and mumble absolute 'nothings' sweetly
through hockey-puck shifted teeth
his smile floating in scars.

So when he came shambling across the barroom floor
it was not for lack of drunkenness
nor for the severely limited intellect
he'd worn like a badge of honor all his days,
but it was for
the 'irrefutable esteem,'
the 'high regard'
the 'deeply felt reverence,'
for the – 'weaker' sex,
that he bowed with the grace of a supplicant
and asked the 'fat broad,'
or so he yclept her
being the only available femme in the joint …
yes, asked her to trip the planks with him
and, upon rejection,
it was 'without malice' for any 'Alice'
that he jiggered his spat-out dental plate
in their station
lodged as they were deep
in his beer glass,
and said to her, mustering a quasi-chivalric grin,

'I don't wanna hump!
I jes wanna dance!'
And, oh, with such heart-melting poetry
she could barely resist
leaping into his arms
and wrapping her ample thighs
about him
craving, as she was, his 'sidewinder.'

Tilting his cap
he swished into the washroom
jarring the frame as he went
and – splashing the best part of the afternoon
on the tiles
made a better pillow of the toilet bowl
than Jacob of his stone
where he dreamed of 'mother' in her apron
togged in slippers
bringing him soup, and the promise of love.

It seemed a sweet enough Evening

It seemed a sweet enough evening
with the air cool and empty all the way from the parking lot
to the stars,
but mist rising from the ice in the arena
like fog on the moors
was gothic.

It hung in the air
and clung to the skaters' dissolving frames.

Is it any wonder the puck leapt
at George's face
the moment he touched the surface?
Struck him flat
so he fell
unable to claw away the gnarled hurt.

Or Gill, who took too close a look
at the blade of a stick,
scratching the bone-china smoothness of his cornea.

Or Frank who twisted his ankle
so it puffed in his boot
like a bull frog in rut.

Or tall Bruce who tripped
and timbered like a Sequoia
bringing down a forest of skaters.

Or John whose smallest finger
sprang against the boards
and snapped backwards in his glove
like a brittle twig.

So you learn to trust the signs.
The crude pathos of team-mates
that crowd the crumpled injury,
the vapor rising from a blood-beribboned nose,
the grimace
when a bone winces in a stocking,

the sudden cold rolled-back look
when the brain yields to a hurt
and drops a player in a slack lump.

But where was the prophesy
on the face of this night
when the moon was shining
like God's own M.V.P.
and the parking lot
was spooky with our footfalls
that rang in the clean air
like vesper bells?
Where was the meaning
we could have read
that would have warned us
about this particular game
fraught with our troubles,
this game where we travelled unwittingly
like a gay carnival of targets?

Gap-toothed Barbarians

His wet hockey equipment
spread on the dressing-room floor
like a gutted deer,
I try to figure
why he hates me.

I've done nothing to offend
this tiny athlete
with the gone-away teeth.

Without comment I've watched him
thrive on the missed glory
of the almost talented.
I've observed him
slobbering unmolested in his corner
reliving a done shot
or the quick thrill
of mediocrity steeped in its puny victories.

Still he slams me into the boards
where I dribble like spit
and I suffer his ridicule
though I know the consequence
of my own unintended ineptitude on ice,
to be shunned like a voice culled from a choir
even then I wonder why
he comes at me
streaking as an unresolved and fierce
muck-up from the primordial gene-pool
of his own ancestral stew
abandoned on the threshold of evolution.
I am polite. I give him room.
I am silent in the face of his oblique jaw-wag.
I do not know…
or perhaps I refuse to accept
the proof of what I know.

That smallness most becomes what it becomes
when it is truly small.

Until the Game was done

Full of tournament hootch
his skates tickety ticking on cement
he wobbled
greenly boozed behind the hockey bench
spitting a kind of bear sperm in his wake
after it gathered in mucusy bunches
upon his gums
and collar-high with bile
he swirled like a ten-button shirt
dropped from a balcony.

But when he was ready
he burst through the gate
and though the puck slurred on his stick
and though he tilted
like a wagging needle dropped by a clumsy nurse
when it's already pricked in the flesh
and (whichever the more heroic act:
      to be drunk and have scored
      or have scored and be drunk)
still he shot and scored
when his face was as green as the cud
of a grass-fed cow
and his smile broke free
from a woozy grimace like an eggshell king
fixed wrong
and a toothless belch
lifted in one brumous wash from his victorious gut.

Busride to and from the
Wheatley-Weekend Hockey Tournament

the going

Away from the voluptuous drumlins of Brant
and the tobacco kilns
that smoke Norfolk skylines
through the blue-blood forest city outskirts
to where doomed cattle caterwaul in Talbotville
down the runnels of Tecumseh country
to the flat orchard bed of Cedar Springs
where the land stretches
a tight drumskin
along the highway in the shadow of lake sky
blue as the eyelid of a sleeping woman
we rattled on our broken bus
a hockey team
smoking cheap cigars, drinking beer,
playing cards, belching and flatulating
the air delicious with manstink
and loud as a boxcar full of market hogs.

Once we stood strung out beneath the bus windows
whizzing in the roadside gravel
the streaking yellow uric ribbons
caught and flung in a gust like frayed skate laces
while the driver for a joke pulled fifty yards uproad
leaving us
our sudden nakedness tonguing
the final embarrassed tears
before we hiked our flies
and ran laughing for the journey's end.

And few could capture the fun in its flight
outdistanced by motions of time and place
where we sang in an off-key chorus
outside as we were of the selves we had brought
to keep the world in.

the coming hence

Two days later riding
back from the rink we sat
some, loose-skinned hounds flung in their seats
suffering the slats
whining and dreaming of the hunt.
And some poisoned the air
with their black-bowelled effulgence
the faithful sulphurous peep of bubbling
subterranean volcanic mud
erupting every half mile.
And some stared blind to the landscape
as if to a 'beyondness' they'd been brought overclose.
And some drank Cap'in Morgan dark rum
till there was naught but a sniff
in the mickey.
And some focussed on the fiery gut length
of what they had done.
And some lions yawned on the veldt
in the monkey-puzzle shade
reliving the kill and fat with it.
But one it seemed
gathered it in
though he had not known it was an elegy
to a dead time
until he wrote it.

The Mystery of Lambs

When the puck hit him in the pills he fell writhing
like a lizard with a steak knife through his head
his body convulsing at the groin
bent there till it finally curled a small knuckle
around a big coin
still as if asleep then death slackened
he shivered himself out straight
turned and drooping on his rising frame
he hobbled to the bench
making adjustments to humility so curious
you'd swear he concealed and cocked
a complicated gun
between his legs
without the benefit of hands.

And there he sat a sea-sick measure
– a grimace throbbing on his face
while the heart regained its sweet perfection
by smoothing out the pulse of pain
that tuned its note upon a tired nerve
played out its pan-pipe theme in quiet pools
relaxing every wildness in the dark
bringing even famous lions down to drink
the music in
as if their brains had been seduced
by the gentle mystery of lambs.

Baby Powder

After every hockey game he plays
he showers
then sprinkles himself with baby powder
so it pollinates his naked skin
and little damp foot plashes
make a poor detective of the floor.

But no one dares to challenge his machismo
for he carries a knife
and one suspects he 'nose-slits' in his best dreams.

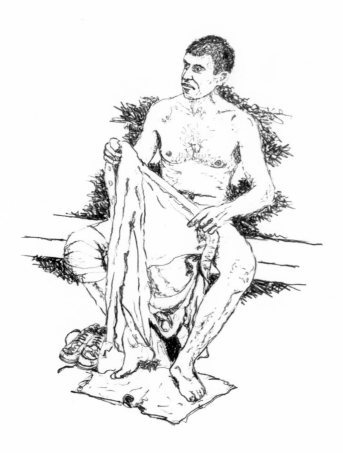

Sliding through a Strangler's Hands

The air was as smoky
as a gambler's train car
on the hockey bench
by coach Jim whose cigarette flared
like a ruby held up to the light
and the fume
rolled in a smothering blanket
over each winded player
blinking eye salt
so it flicked like ash
from a sacred fire.

Jim waved the thing in the air
gesticulating, an artist
painting blood on a huge canvas
and it fogged each pure precious molecule of oxygen.

I would have plucked the burning tobacco tit
like a sun-hot berry
and flung the fiery ingot
printing a sizzling divot on the rink
– a cat hiss cooled by sanctuary.

But I was raised on manners
so I kept objections private
gasping quietly
seizing the difficult air
that entered by lungs like a pale blue scarf
sliding through strangler's hands.

Lucky Life

My politics and my hockey are both left wing
though I would not
raise a gun for either
nor snipe from the safety of my lucky life.

Bad men make such easy targets
shaping broken grammar with their mouths
while they quarrel with a skatelace
that sets porridged in an eyelet
too snug for moving either way,
thus are their arguments
locked and fisted in the tight clean
chambers of the mind.

Let them arrive
armed against gentleness –
I will sit for hours
rocking my blade against a board
waiting to play.

Yet I will not come mean for any man
though he catch me at my vespers
like a Becket priest
or threaten my better army of words
with a thousand
inarticulate silences.

The Ritual

When D fights on the ice
he has a ritual
disrobing like a priest
first he puts his gloves down one by one
unsnaps his helmet
and sets it carefully on the surface
like fragile pottery
then he assumes a stance
as if posing
his form sculpted, fists curled and professional
eyes cold and narrow.

Usually the intended's rage fails
like a whistling kettle lifted from a flame
or the opponent
might paw the air like a bear
crazy with blackflies
before he gives D an 'ahh – not worth it' look and swat.

But if he decides instead
to come at D
D just grabs the fellow's sweater
and pulls it up over his head
so he's ridiculous as a half-shorn sheep.

You learn to cold-cock D mid-play
or you learn to leave him alone.
Either way D almost always wins.

Stitching in Stone

When body
has left the long honeymoon
of the hand
to find true manhood
in a dressing-room after a game
where sweat plits
on skate tops like the first spit
of sickly summer rain
these men
make a vulgar distance from their wives
travelling to where a woman
is merely pluggable –
a thing to be puttied over
and trowelled flat
by the urgency of the groin
and the imagined fractious needle pricks of quick sex
as if they were stitching
in stone.

Then they move for the showers
naked, jostling like bulls, genitalic
exclamation marks unhinged and hanging
half-scissored from a sentence
without imperatives.
Pale and ridiculous they stand
in the lacerating water,
in the strong dumb pulse of undrinkably soapy life.

Injuries

Upper lip, sliced
along the line of the philtrum
to the base of the nose –
two teeth liberated.

Ankle, shattered
like a dropped ice cube.

Cornea, scratched
like a junk man's tea cup.

Puck glances
from a skull ... eyes flutter
body drops
like an overcoat too heavy for a nail.

Wind, knocked out, gasping
like a piper's first note.

Leave a blood trail to the dressing-room
wounded beast,
hand cupped over
the halved apricot of a nose.

On his Birthday he slammed Two-footed

i

He slammed two-footed
into the hockey boards
and shattered his tibia
above the ankle.

His nerves jangled
like cheap salvation tambourines
and fired up his leg
blazing the jingles and popping the tacks
stoking past the knee
so he squinted to read the pained print
on the burning page
of his bone
corn-stalked in the flesh
and pushed pistonning up the shin
so bone swallowed bone
furculating and splintering
like something dog-crunched.

And in that instant
when he softened the shaft
so it whipped in the middle
like an actor's rapier
took a year
and couched it – made of his foot
a snooty cushion cat
and buried his mind in books,
bad television,
and a most profound regret.

ii

After the incident
his skates sat empty on the dressing-room floor
husked of their fruit
like Kemmerich's boots
while he lay
blazing on the stretcher bed
in emergency
his leg wrapped in bathing-caps of crushed ice
blue as midnight frost.

Tall Bruce falling in a Hockey Game

He falls unhinging from his feet
and takes two skaters
with him
like a tree
falling among trees.

Some of the same
creaking and cracking as he goes down
and we listen
almost lumberjacks
in the dangerous timbering moments
of his romance
with gravity
hockey sticks flying in the air
like knocked-off branches

and after the clattering demise
of his weighty long-boned, slow-motion imperative –

the unbelievable
awestruck
hush of birds.

Dying on the Ice at 39 is Hard

He stepped onto the ice
circled twice
fell flat   and died.

No Shakesperean monologues.
No dying words for a desperate son.
No pyrotechnics of the heart.
It just suddenly stopped
like a small bird slamming into glass.

His teammates gathered
in a stunned huddle
then breathed away from him
on worried skates
that day they tore their calendars
like grieving widows.

He went cold so fast
his pulse stuck on the half beat
like a swirling coin under a gambler's thumb
and he lay in a limp heap.

Whether November moves in the bones of a tree
or April is coral coloured with crocus
sea-shelled in a tiny garden
death comes when death comes
and 'he was dead when he hit the ice'
but dying on the ice at 39 is hard.

On the busride home
they carried his corpse
in the beer cooler
and drank quietly
like buck-deer in a moonlit clearing
thinking about what everyone who has ever lived
is too stupid to understand.

My Father quit Hockey one Night Late in his Youth

My father quit hockey
one night late in his youth.
Went home
and hung his skates in the shed
told his young bride
he was done with the game.

Done with the time he would race
a catalogue bent round each shin
and the wind in his face.
Done with the crack of the puck
and the rush-cut of the blade.
Done with the music of heart in the head.
Done with the sanguine age
when winter had a joy to rival the summer's sun.

He still tells the story
of one luckless player
who lived out his days a broken doll
heart quietly ticking
like a great clock lost in a corner.

But as for me
I feel a sadness that cannot grieve
and like a wicked son
I risk unmendable memory
and play the game beyond
the reach of wisdom in my ever collapsing years.

Look at the Stars

The kexes of the field
are broken under foot
and breathed
with snow
like dusty flutes
of filthy bottle mouths
that reed melancholy notes
in winter wind.

Here boys
who drown their socks
in ice
have come to skate
their faces red
and happy as the mood of streams

but later
when they shake their hats
and move indoors
to chocolate steam
then
a howling lonely-dogs the window ledge
or skifts
the distance
where they were
like mirrors in an empty house
the walls fallen on their bricks
to look at the stars.